The Secret

Understanding These Fascinating Creatures

The information provided in this book is intended for educational and informational purposes only. It is not intended to be a substitute for professional advice or treatment.

The author and publisher of this book are not responsible for any errors or omissions in the content, or for any consequences resulting from the use of the information provided in this book. The author and publisher do not endorse any specific products or services mentioned in this book.

Readers should consult with a qualified professional before making any decisions or taking any actions based on the information provided in this book. The author and publisher specifically disclaim any liability for any damages or losses incurred by any person or entity as a result of the use or misuse of the information provided in this book.

Book Introduction

Moles are creatures of mystery, spending much of their lives underground, hidden from sight. Their subterranean lifestyle has made them the subject of much fascination and curiosity, yet they remain little understood by most people. In this book, we'll take you on a journey into the secret world of moles, exploring their unique physical characteristics, behaviors, and habitats.

We'll also delve into the important roles moles play in their ecosystem, their impact on human activities, and the challenges they face in the modern world. From their adaptation to life underground to their complex social interactions, moles are fascinating creatures that offer much to explore and discover.

We'll bring you up close and personal with these elusive animals, providing a window into their world that few have ever seen. We'll also explore the cultural significance of moles throughout human history, from their roles in mythology and folklore to their place in modern society.

Whether you're a nature enthusiast, a biology student, or simply curious about the natural world, "The Secret World of Moles" is the ultimate guide to understanding these fascinating creatures. So join us as we explore the world of moles and unlock the secrets of their hidden world.

The World of Moles: Introduction

Moles are small, furry creatures that are known for their subterranean lifestyle. They are found in various parts of the world, including North America, Europe, and Asia. Moles are highly specialized animals that are adapted to living underground, and their unique physical characteristics and behaviors are shaped by their environment.

In this chapter, we will introduce you to the world of moles, exploring their habitat, physical characteristics, and behaviors. We'll also look at the different types of moles that exist and how they differ from one another.

Moles are known for their long, cylindrical bodies, which are designed to move easily through the soil. They have short, powerful legs and broad, strong paws that are adapted for digging. Moles are also equipped with sharp claws that allow them to dig quickly and efficiently.

Moles have a highly developed sense of touch, which is essential for navigating their underground environment. They use their sensitive snouts to detect vibrations and changes in pressure, allowing them to locate prey and avoid obstacles. Their eyesight is poor, and they are nearly blind, but their hearing is highly sensitive.

Moles are solitary animals that spend most of their lives underground. They are active day and night, and their activity patterns are often influenced by factors such as temperature, rainfall, and soil conditions. Moles are carnivorous and feed primarily on insects, worms, and other small invertebrates.

There are many different species of moles, each adapted to a specific habitat and environment. The most common type of mole is the Eastern mole, which is found throughout North America. The European mole is another common species that is found throughout Europe and Asia.

In the next chapter, we will take a closer look at the physical characteristics of moles and how they are adapted to their underground lifestyle. We'll explore their unique skeletal structure, as well as their specialized muscles and organs that allow them to dig and move easily through the soil. Join us as we continue our journey into the world of moles.

The Anatomy of a Mole: Understanding Their Physical Characteristics

Moles are unique animals that are adapted to living underground. Their bodies have evolved to allow them to move easily through the soil, hunt for prey, and avoid predators. In this chapter, we will explore the physical characteristics of moles in more detail, looking at their skeletal structure, muscular system, and organs.

One of the most striking features of moles is their long, cylindrical bodies. Their bodies are designed to move through the soil with ease, and their bones are adapted to support their burrowing lifestyle. Moles have strong, flexible spines that allow them to twist and turn as they move through the soil. They also have powerful forelimbs that are adapted for digging.

Moles have a unique skeletal structure that allows them to move easily through the soil. Their bones are dense and heavy, which gives them a greater mass for pushing through the soil. They also have strong muscles that attach to their bones, providing the power necessary for digging and tunneling.

Moles have specialized muscles that allow them to dig with incredible force. Their forelimbs are powerful and heavily muscled, providing the strength needed to dig through tough soil. Moles can dig through the soil at a rate of up to 15 feet per hour, making them some of the most efficient diggers in the animal kingdom.

Moles also have specialized organs that are adapted to their underground lifestyle. Their eyesight is poor, but they have a highly developed sense of touch. Moles have sensitive snouts that are equipped with sensory receptors, allowing them to detect vibrations and changes in pressure. They use this sense of touch to navigate their environment, locate prey, and avoid obstacles.

Moles also have a unique cardiovascular system that is adapted to their underground lifestyle. Their hearts are larger than those of most other mammals, allowing them to pump blood more efficiently. They also have a higher concentration of red blood cells, which helps them to extract more oxygen from the soil.

In the next chapter, we will explore the habitat of moles, looking at the different types of soil and environments where they can be found. We'll also examine the unique adaptations that moles have developed to survive in these environments. Join us as we continue our journey into the world of moles.

The Mole's Habitat: Where Do They Live and Thrive?

Moles are found in a variety of habitats around the world, from grasslands and forests to deserts and wetlands. However, they are most commonly associated with grasslands and farmlands, where the soil is soft and moist, making it easier for them to dig their tunnels. In this chapter, we will explore the different types of habitats where moles can be found and the unique adaptations that allow them to thrive in these environments.

Moles prefer to live in soil that is moist, loose, and easy to dig through. They are found in a variety of soil types, including sandy soil, loamy soil, and clay soil. Moles are also known to prefer soil that is rich in organic matter, as this provides a source of food for the insects and other small invertebrates that they prey upon.

Moles can be found in a variety of habitats, including grasslands, forests, farmlands, and wetlands. In grasslands and farmlands, moles are often associated with the underground burrows that they create. These burrows can cause damage to crops and can be a nuisance to farmers, but they also provide an important habitat for moles and other animals.

In forests, moles are often found in areas with a thick layer of leaf litter or other organic material on the forest floor. These areas provide a source of food for moles and allow them to create tunnels and burrows in the soil.

In wetlands, moles are often found in areas with high water tables. They are adapted to living in these areas, as their burrows are less likely to collapse in the moist soil. Wetlands also provide a rich source of food for moles, as they are home to many insects and other small invertebrates.

Moles have developed a number of unique adaptations that allow them to thrive in these diverse habitats. For example, their powerful forelimbs and sharp claws allow them to dig through tough soil and create burrows and tunnels. Their sense of touch allows them to navigate through their environment, locate prey, and avoid predators.

In the next chapter, we will look at the diet of moles and the different types of prey that they consume. We'll examine the role that moles play in their ecosystem and how their feeding habits impact the environment around them. Join us as we continue our journey into the world of moles.

The Mole's Diet: What Do They Eat?

Moles are carnivores, which means they feed primarily on other animals. Their diet consists mainly of insects, earthworms, and other small invertebrates that they find underground. In this chapter, we will explore the diet of moles in more detail, looking at the different types of prey that they consume and the unique adaptations that allow them to hunt and capture their food.

Moles are adapted to hunting and capturing prey in their underground environment. Their powerful forelimbs and sharp claws allow them to dig through the soil quickly and efficiently, while their sensitive snouts allow them to detect the presence of prey. Once they have located their prey, moles will use their sharp teeth to kill and consume it.

The primary food source for moles is earthworms. Earthworms are a rich source of protein and other nutrients, and they are abundant in many types of soil. Moles are able to locate earthworms by detecting the vibrations that they make as they move through the soil.

In addition to earthworms, moles also feed on a variety of other small invertebrates, including insects, grubs, and larvae. They may also occasionally feed on small vertebrates, such as mice and shrews.

Moles have a high metabolism, which means they need to eat frequently to maintain their energy levels. They may consume up to 80% of their body weight in food each day. This means that they are constantly on the hunt for prey, and their underground burrows and tunnels provide them with easy access to their food sources.

The feeding habits of moles can have a significant impact on their environment. By consuming large numbers of earthworms and other small invertebrates, moles can help to regulate the populations of these organisms. They can also help to aerate the soil and improve its quality by creating tunnels and burrows.

However, the burrowing habits of moles can also have a negative impact on their environment. Their burrows can damage crops and other vegetation, and they can create holes and tunnels that can be hazardous to livestock and other animals.

In the next chapter, we will explore the senses of moles in more detail, looking at the unique adaptations that allow them to navigate their environment and locate prey. Join us as we continue our journey into the world of moles.

The Mole's Senses: How Do They Perceive the World Around Them?

Moles live in a dark and subterranean environment, and their senses have evolved to help them navigate and hunt in this unique habitat. In this chapter, we will explore the senses of moles in more detail, looking at the unique adaptations that allow them to perceive the world around them.

Moles have poor eyesight and are nearly blind. This is because their underground environment is mostly devoid of light. However, their sense of touch is highly developed, and they use this sense to navigate and hunt in their environment.

Moles have sensitive snouts that are equipped with sensory receptors. These receptors allow them to detect vibrations and changes in pressure, which they use to navigate their environment and locate prey. Moles can detect the presence of earthworms and other small invertebrates by the vibrations that they make as they move through the soil.

Moles also have a highly developed sense of smell, which they use to locate prey and navigate their environment. Their sense of smell is particularly important when it comes to locating prey that is buried deep in the soil, such as earthworms and other small invertebrates.

In addition to their sense of touch and smell, moles also have a highly sensitive sense of hearing. This allows them to detect the sounds of predators or other potential threats in their environment. Their ears are small and located close to their head, which allows them to detect sounds that are close by.

Moles have a number of unique adaptations that allow them to perceive the world around them. For example, their eyes are small and located deep in their skulls, which protects them from damage as they dig through the soil. Their sense of touch is highly developed, which allows them to navigate their environment and locate prey.

Moles also have a number of specialized muscles and organs that allow them to dig through the soil and create burrows and tunnels. These adaptations include powerful forelimbs, sharp claws, and a unique skeletal structure that allows them to twist and turn as they move through the soil.

In the next chapter, we will explore the behavior of moles in more detail, looking at the unique habits and social interactions of these fascinating animals. Join us as we continue our journey into the world of moles.

The Behavior of Moles: How Do They Live and Interact?

Moles are solitary animals that spend most of their lives underground. They are adapted to living in their subterranean environment, and their behavior is shaped by their unique habitat. In this chapter, we will explore the behavior of moles in more detail, looking at their unique habits and social interactions.

Moles are solitary animals, and they typically only interact with other moles during the breeding season. However, some species of moles are known to be more social than others. For example, the Townsend's mole in North America has been observed living in large underground colonies.

Moles are active day and night, and their activity patterns are influenced by a variety of factors, including temperature, rainfall, and soil conditions. They are most active during the spring and fall, when soil moisture levels are high and temperatures are moderate.

Moles are adapted to living underground, and their behavior is shaped by their subterranean lifestyle. They create complex networks of tunnels and burrows, which they use for shelter, hunting, and navigation. They also use their tunnels to store food and to mark their territory.

Moles are carnivorous, and they feed primarily on earthworms and other small invertebrates that they find underground. They are constantly on the hunt for prey, and their burrowing habits allow them to quickly and efficiently locate and capture their food.

Moles also play an important role in their ecosystem. By consuming large numbers of earthworms and other small invertebrates, they can help to regulate the populations of these organisms. They can also help to aerate the soil and improve its quality by creating tunnels and burrows.

However, the burrowing habits of moles can also have a negative impact on their environment. Their burrows can damage crops and other vegetation, and they can create holes and tunnels that can be hazardous to livestock and other animals.

In the next chapter, we will explore the different types of moles that exist and how they differ from one another. We'll look at their physical characteristics, behavior, and habitat, providing a comprehensive overview of the fascinating world of moles. Join us as we continue our journey into the world of moles.

The Different Types of Moles: A Comprehensive Overview

Moles are found all over the world, and there are many different species that exist. Each species of mole has its own unique physical characteristics, behavior, and habitat. In this chapter, we will explore the different types of moles that exist and how they differ from one another.

There are several different families of moles, including Talpidae, which includes most of the world's moles, and Chrysochloridae, which includes the golden moles of Africa. Within these families, there are many different species of moles, each with its own unique characteristics.

One of the most common species of mole is the eastern mole, which is found in eastern North America. Eastern moles have dark brown or black fur and a pointed snout that is equipped with sensory receptors. They are known for their burrowing habits and their ability to dig through tough soil.

Another common species of mole is the European mole, which is found throughout Europe and parts of Asia. European moles have gray-brown fur and a cylindrical body that is adapted for burrowing. They are known for their powerful forelimbs and sharp claws, which they use to dig through the soil.

The star-nosed mole is another species of mole that is found in North America. These moles have a distinctive star-shaped snout that is covered in sensory receptors. They use their sense of touch to locate prey, which they consume in large quantities.

Golden moles, which are found in Africa, are a unique group of moles that are adapted to living in arid and semi-arid habitats. They have cylindrical bodies and short, powerful limbs that allow them to burrow through the hard soil. They are known for their sharp claws and their ability to detect prey through vibrations in the soil.

In addition to these species, there are many other types of moles that exist around the world, each with its own unique characteristics and adaptations. By studying the different types of moles, we can gain a greater understanding of these fascinating animals and their role in their ecosystems.

In the next chapter, we will explore the conservation status of moles and the threats that they face in the wild. We'll look at the efforts being made to protect these animals and their habitats, and what we can do to help. Join us as we continue our journey into the world of moles.

The Conservation of Moles: Protecting These Fascinating Animals

Moles play an important role in their ecosystems, and they are a fascinating and unique group of animals. However, many species of moles are facing threats in the wild, including habitat loss, pollution, and climate change. In this chapter, we will explore the conservation status of moles and the efforts being made to protect them.

Many species of moles are considered to be of least concern by the International Union for Conservation of Nature (IUCN). However, several species are considered to be endangered or vulnerable. For example, the Russian desman, a type of mole found in Russia and parts of Asia, is considered to be critically endangered due to habitat loss and pollution.

Habitat loss is one of the primary threats facing moles in the wild. As human populations continue to expand, more and more land is being developed for agriculture, housing, and other purposes. This can lead to the destruction of natural habitats, making it more difficult for moles and other animals to survive.

Pollution is another threat to moles in the wild. Chemical pollutants, such as pesticides and herbicides, can accumulate in the soil and can have a negative impact on the health of moles and other animals. Climate change is also a concern, as it can lead to changes in the availability of water and food, which can impact the survival of moles and other animals.

Efforts are being made to protect moles and their habitats. One of the most important ways to protect moles is to preserve their natural habitats. This can be done through the establishment of protected areas, such as national parks and wildlife reserves. In addition, efforts are being made to reduce pollution and to promote sustainable agricultural practices.

There is also a need for more research on moles and their habitats. By studying these animals, we can gain a greater understanding of their behavior, biology, and ecology. This information can then be used to develop effective conservation strategies.

In addition to these efforts, individuals can also play a role in protecting moles and their habitats. This can be done by supporting conservation organizations, reducing the use of chemicals in the garden, and planting native plants that provide food and habitat for moles and other animals.

By working together, we can help to protect these fascinating animals and ensure that they continue to play an important role in their ecosystems for generations to come.

Moles in Culture and Mythology

Throughout history, moles have played a role in the cultures and mythologies of many different societies. From symbols of good luck and fertility to creatures of darkness and deceit, moles have been associated with a variety of different meanings and interpretations. In this chapter, we will explore the role of moles in culture and mythology.

In many cultures, moles have been associated with good luck and fertility. In Chinese culture, for example, moles are seen as a symbol of good fortune, and it is believed that having a mole on certain parts of the body can bring luck and prosperity. In European folklore, moles were sometimes associated with fertility, and it was believed that touching a mole's fur could help women conceive.

In other cultures, moles have been seen as creatures of darkness and deceit. In Native American mythology, for example, moles were sometimes associated with death and the underworld. In some African cultures, moles were associated with witchcraft and dark magic.

Moles have also played a role in literature and art. In the children's book "The Wind in the Willows," the character Mole is one of the main protagonists. The book portrays moles as friendly, curious creatures who are fascinated by the world around them.

In addition to their cultural and mythological significance, moles have also played an important role in scientific research. The study of moles has helped scientists to better understand the biology and behavior of burrowing animals, as well as the structure and function of the sensory organs.

Overall, moles have been a source of fascination and intrigue throughout human history. From symbols of good luck and fertility to creatures of darkness and deceit, moles have been associated with a wide variety of meanings and interpretations. By exploring the role of moles in culture and mythology, we can gain a greater appreciation for these fascinating animals and their place in the world around us.

Living with Moles: How to Coexist with These Fascinating Animals

Moles can be fascinating animals to observe, but they can also be a nuisance for homeowners and gardeners. Their burrowing habits can damage lawns, gardens, and other landscaping, and their presence can be frustrating for those who want to maintain a pristine yard. In this chapter, we will explore ways to coexist with moles and minimize the impact of their burrowing.

One way to minimize the impact of moles is to create a barrier between your lawn or garden and the soil. This can be done by installing a barrier made of hardware cloth or similar material around the perimeter of your yard or garden. The barrier should be buried at least a foot deep to prevent moles from burrowing underneath it.

Another way to coexist with moles is to modify your landscaping to make it less attractive to them. This can be done by removing excess thatch from your lawn, which can provide moles with a source of food and shelter. You can also avoid overwatering your lawn, as moist soil is more attractive to moles than dry soil.

If you have a persistent mole problem, you may want to consider using traps or repellents to discourage their activity. Traps can be effective in capturing and removing moles from your property, while repellents can be used to create an unpleasant environment for moles, discouraging them from burrowing in your lawn or garden.

It is important to remember that moles play an important role in their ecosystems, and they are a valuable part of the natural world. While it may be frustrating to deal with their burrowing habits, it is important to take a humane and responsible approach to managing their presence.

By coexisting with moles and taking steps to minimize the impact of their burrowing, you can enjoy the presence of these fascinating animals while maintaining a beautiful and healthy yard or garden.

Moles and Their Importance in Agriculture

While moles can be a nuisance for homeowners and gardeners, they also play an important role in agriculture. The burrowing habits of moles can help to aerate soil and improve its quality, making it more fertile and productive. In this chapter, we will explore the importance of moles in agriculture and how their presence can benefit farmers and gardeners.

Moles are known for their burrowing habits, which can create tunnels and burrows that help to aerate the soil. This process can improve soil structure and increase water infiltration, allowing plant roots to grow more deeply and access more nutrients. In addition, the tunnels and burrows created by moles can provide a habitat for other beneficial organisms, such as earthworms and microorganisms, which can further improve soil health.

The presence of moles in agricultural fields can also have a positive impact on crop yields. By improving soil quality, moles can help to increase the productivity of crops, resulting in higher yields and better quality produce. In addition, the presence of moles can help to reduce soil compaction, which can improve the health of plant roots and increase their ability to absorb nutrients.

While moles are not typically considered a beneficial species in agriculture, their presence can have a positive impact on the health and productivity of crops. By improving soil quality and reducing soil compaction, moles can help to create a more sustainable and productive agricultural system.

However, it is important to manage the presence of moles in agricultural fields to prevent damage to crops and other plants. Farmers and gardeners can use a variety of methods to manage the presence of moles, including installing barriers and repellents, modifying irrigation practices, and using traps to capture and remove moles from the area.

By understanding the importance of moles in agriculture and taking steps to manage their presence in a responsible way, farmers and gardeners can benefit from the positive impact of these fascinating animals on their crops and the environment.

The Future of Moles: Challenges and Opportunities

As we continue to learn more about moles and their role in the world around us, we are faced with a number of challenges and opportunities for their conservation and management. In this chapter, we will explore some of the key issues facing moles today and how we can work to ensure their future.

One of the main challenges facing moles today is habitat loss and fragmentation. As human populations continue to expand and landscapes are developed for agriculture and urbanization, the natural habitats of moles are being destroyed or fragmented. This can lead to a decline in populations and make it more difficult for moles to find suitable habitat and resources.

Another challenge facing moles is pollution and climate change. Chemical pollutants, such as pesticides and herbicides, can have a negative impact on the health of moles and their prey, while climate change can alter the availability of water and food resources. These factors can impact the survival of moles and their ability to adapt to changing environmental conditions.

Despite these challenges, there are also opportunities for the conservation and management of moles. One such opportunity is the development of sustainable agricultural practices that can minimize the impact of farming on the natural habitats of moles. This can include the use of organic and low-impact farming methods that preserve soil health and biodiversity.

Another opportunity is the development of conservation programs and initiatives that focus on the protection and restoration of mole habitats. These programs can include the establishment of protected areas, habitat restoration projects, and public education and outreach efforts.

In addition, there is a need for more research on moles and their ecology. By studying these animals, we can gain a greater understanding of their behavior, biology, and role in their ecosystems. This information can then be used to develop effective conservation and management strategies.

Overall, the future of moles depends on our ability to manage their presence in a responsible and sustainable way. By addressing the challenges facing moles today and seizing the opportunities for conservation and management, we can ensure a bright future for these fascinating animals and the ecosystems they inhabit.

Moles in Popular Culture

Moles have long been a source of inspiration for popular culture, appearing in literature, film, television, and other forms of media. From children's books to horror movies, moles have been used to convey a wide range of meanings and emotions. In this chapter, we will explore the role of moles in popular culture and how they have been portrayed in different media.

One of the most famous representations of moles in popular culture is the character of Mole in the children's book "The Wind in the Willows" by Kenneth Grahame. Mole is a curious and adventurous character who explores the world around him with enthusiasm and wonder. The character of Mole has become a beloved icon of children's literature and has been adapted into many different forms of media, including movies, television shows, and video games.

In horror movies and other forms of dark fiction, moles have been used to convey a sense of foreboding and unease. In the horror movie "The Burrowers," moles are depicted as monstrous creatures that terrorize a group of travelers in the Old West. In other works of horror fiction, moles have been used as symbols of darkness and evil, representing the primal and instinctual aspects of human nature.

In popular music, moles have been referenced in a number of different songs, often as a metaphor for something hidden or buried. For example, the song "Dig a Little Deeper" by the band Peter Bjorn and John features the lyrics "Dig a little deeper, find a little mole / Buried in the ground, don't let it take its toll." The metaphor of the mole as something hidden or buried can be a powerful tool for conveying emotions and ideas in music and other forms of media.

Overall, moles have played a diverse and multifaceted role in popular culture, serving as symbols of curiosity, fear, and mystery. By exploring the ways in which moles have been represented in different forms of media, we can gain a greater appreciation for their cultural significance and the role they play in our collective imagination.

Moles in Art and Design

Moles have also been a popular subject in the world of art and design. From paintings to sculptures, jewelry to fashion, moles have been used as a source of inspiration for many artists and designers throughout history. In this chapter, we will explore the role of moles in art and design and how they have been incorporated into different forms of creative expression.

Moles have also been incorporated into contemporary art and design, appearing in a variety of different forms and media. In sculpture, moles have been used as a subject for both representational and abstract works, ranging from realistic depictions of the animal to stylized interpretations. In jewelry and fashion design, moles have been used as a source of inspiration for unique and creative pieces, incorporating elements of their appearance and behavior into the design.

In addition to their aesthetic appeal, moles have also been used as a symbol of environmental conservation and sustainability in art and design. By incorporating moles into their work, artists and designers can draw attention to the importance of preserving the natural habitats of these animals and the ecosystems they inhabit.

Overall, moles have played a significant role in the world of art and design, serving as a source of inspiration for artists and designers across a wide range of disciplines. By exploring the ways in which moles have been incorporated into different forms of creative expression, we can gain a greater appreciation for their cultural significance and their place in the world around us.

The Ethics of Mole Management

As we continue to coexist with moles and manage their presence in our yards, gardens, and agricultural fields, we are faced with ethical questions and considerations. How do we balance our desire to maintain a healthy and productive environment with the need to respect the natural habitats and behaviors of moles? In this chapter, we will explore the ethics of mole management and the different approaches that can be taken to minimize the impact of their burrowing.

One ethical consideration in mole management is the use of lethal methods, such as traps and poisons, to control their populations. While these methods can be effective in removing moles from an area, they also pose a risk to other animals and can be harmful to the environment. It is important to use these methods responsibly and in accordance with local laws and regulations.

Another ethical consideration is the impact of mole management on the natural habitats and behaviors of these animals. While it may be tempting to remove moles from an area to protect our landscaping or crops, it is important to consider the impact this can have on their survival and the health of the ecosystems they inhabit. It may be necessary to modify our landscaping and agricultural practices to coexist with moles in a more sustainable way.

One approach to mole management that is both effective and ethical is the use of non-lethal methods, such as barriers and repellents, to discourage their burrowing. These methods can be effective in minimizing the impact of moles on our landscaping and agricultural fields without harming the animals themselves. In addition, non-lethal methods can be used in combination with other management strategies, such as habitat restoration and public education, to create a more holistic and sustainable approach to mole management.

Ultimately, the ethics of mole management depend on our ability to balance our desire to maintain a healthy and productive environment with our responsibility to respect the natural habitats and behaviors of moles. By taking a humane and responsible approach to mole management, we can minimize the impact of their burrowing while protecting their place in the natural world.

The Benefits of Learning About Moles

Learning about moles and their behavior can provide a number of benefits, both in terms of personal enjoyment and environmental conservation. In this chapter, we will explore some of the benefits of learning about moles and how this knowledge can be applied to improve our lives and the world around us.

One benefit of learning about moles is the opportunity to observe and appreciate their fascinating behavior. By understanding the natural history and behavior of moles, we can better appreciate their role in the ecosystems they inhabit and gain a greater appreciation for the natural world. Observing moles in their natural habitat can be a source of personal enjoyment and a way to connect with nature.

Another benefit of learning about moles is the opportunity to apply this knowledge to environmental conservation and management. By understanding the impact of moles on the environment and the ways in which their behavior can be managed, we can develop more sustainable and effective management strategies. This can include the use of non-lethal management methods, habitat restoration, and public education efforts.

In addition, learning about moles can provide educational opportunities for children and adults alike. By studying these fascinating animals, we can gain a greater understanding of biology, ecology, and environmental science. This knowledge can be applied to a wide range of fields, from agriculture and landscaping to conservation and wildlife management.

Overall, the benefits of learning about moles extend beyond personal enjoyment and can have a positive impact on the environment and the world around us. By understanding the natural history and behavior of these fascinating animals, we can develop more sustainable and effective management strategies and gain a greater appreciation for the natural world.

Top Questions About Moles Answered

In this chapter, we will answer some of the most common questions about moles, providing readers with a comprehensive understanding of these fascinating animals.

1. What are moles? Moles are small, burrowing mammals that belong to the Talpidae family.
2. What do moles look like? Moles are typically small and round with short, velvety fur. They have small eyes and ears, and long, pointed snouts.
3. What is the lifespan of a mole? Moles typically live for 2-3 years in the wild.
4. What do moles eat? Moles primarily eat earthworms and other soil invertebrates.
5. Why do moles burrow? Moles burrow to create tunnels and burrows that provide them with shelter and access to food.
6. Are moles harmful to humans? Moles are not harmful to humans, but their burrowing habits can damage lawns and gardens.
7. How do you get rid of moles in your yard? There are a variety of methods for managing mole populations, including the use of traps, barriers, and repellents.
8. What is a molehill? A molehill is a mound of earth that is created by moles as they dig tunnels and burrows.
9. Can moles swim? Moles are not strong swimmers, but they can swim short distances if necessary.

10. Do moles have any natural predators? Moles have a number of natural predators, including owls, hawks, and snakes.
11. Are moles blind? Moles have small eyes that are adapted for low-light conditions, but they are not blind.
12. How fast can moles dig? Moles can dig up to 18 feet per hour.
13. How deep do moles burrow? Moles typically burrow between 3 and 12 inches below the surface of the soil.
14. What is a mole's role in the ecosystem? Moles play an important role in the ecosystem by aerating soil and providing a habitat for other beneficial organisms.
15. How many species of moles are there? There are over 40 species of moles found throughout the world.
16. How do moles communicate? Moles communicate through scent and touch, using their sense of smell and specialized hairs on their bodies to navigate their environment.
17. Do moles hibernate? Moles do not hibernate, but they may become less active during periods of extreme cold or heat.
18. Can moles cause damage to crops? Moles can damage crops by creating tunnels and burrows that disturb soil structure and reduce soil quality.
19. Do moles have any economic importance? Moles can have economic importance in agriculture, where their burrowing habits can improve soil quality and increase crop yields.
20. How can you tell if moles are present in your yard? Moles are typically indicated by the presence of molehills and tunnels in the soil.

21. What is the gestation period of a mole? The gestation period of a mole is typically around 4-6 weeks.
22. Do moles have any social behavior? Moles are typically solitary animals and do not display social behavior.
23. How do moles mate? Moles mate in underground burrows, typically during the spring and summer months.
24. Can moles see in the dark? Moles have adapted to low-light conditions but do not have night vision.
25. How do moles avoid predators? Moles rely on their ability to burrow and their sense of smell to avoid predators.

26. How do moles affect soil quality? Moles can improve soil quality by aerating the soil and mixing organic matter into the top layer, which can promote plant growth.
27. Can moles be beneficial for gardens? Moles can be beneficial for gardens by improving soil quality and reducing pest populations, but their burrowing habits can also damage plant roots.
28. Can moles carry diseases? Moles are not known to carry diseases that are transmissible to humans.
29. How can you discourage moles from burrowing in your yard? There are a number of methods for discouraging moles from burrowing in your yard, including the use of physical barriers, applying repellents, and modifying landscaping practices to create less favorable habitat conditions.

Conclusion

Moles are fascinating animals that play an important role in the ecosystems they inhabit. While their burrowing habits can be frustrating for homeowners and farmers, it is important to understand and respect the natural behaviors and habitats of moles in order to manage their populations in a sustainable and ethical way.

Throughout this book, we have explored the natural history and behavior of moles, as well as their impact on the environment and ways in which they can be managed. From their unique adaptations for life underground to their important role in soil health, moles are a fascinating and important part of the natural world.

As we continue to coexist with moles and manage their presence in our yards and agricultural fields, it is important to take a humane and responsible approach to mole management. By incorporating non-lethal methods, such as barriers and repellents, and modifying our landscaping and agricultural practices to create more favorable habitat conditions, we can minimize the impact of moles on our surroundings while respecting their place in the natural world.

Overall, the study of moles provides us with a greater appreciation for the complexity and diversity of the natural world, as well as the importance of environmental conservation and sustainability. Whether you are a homeowner, farmer, or simply a nature enthusiast, learning about moles can provide a rewarding and informative experience that will deepen your understanding of the world around us.

Epilogue

In conclusion, the study of moles has provided us with a unique insight into the complexity and diversity of the natural world. From their fascinating adaptations for life underground to their important role in soil health, moles are a remarkable example of the diversity of life on our planet.

As we continue to coexist with moles and manage their presence in our environment, it is important to take a humane and responsible approach to mole management. By incorporating non-lethal methods and modifying our landscaping and agricultural practices to create more favorable habitat conditions, we can minimize the impact of moles on our surroundings while respecting their place in the natural world.

Whether you are a homeowner, farmer, or simply a nature enthusiast, the study of moles provides us with a unique opportunity to deepen our understanding of the natural world and the importance of environmental conservation and sustainability. By embracing this knowledge and incorporating it into our daily lives, we can create a more sustainable and harmonious relationship with the natural world around us.

Author's Note

I hope that this book has provided readers with a comprehensive and informative overview of the fascinating world of moles. As someone who has spent many years studying these remarkable animals, I am continually amazed by their unique adaptations and important role in the natural world.

I believe that it is important for us to not only understand and appreciate the natural world, but to also take responsibility for our impact on it. By incorporating sustainable and responsible mole management practices, we can minimize our impact on the environment while preserving the important ecological functions that moles provide.

I encourage readers to continue learning about moles and their role in the natural world, and to take an active role in promoting sustainable and responsible mole management practices. By working together, we can create a more sustainable and harmonious relationship with the natural world around us.

Thank you for reading, and I hope that this book has been a valuable resource for you.

Printed in Great Britain
by Amazon